# Thomas More

## Faith-Fille

1478–1535
Born in London, England
Feast Day: June 22
Family Connection: Fathers

Text by Barbara Yoffie
Illustrated by Katherine A. Borgatti

## Liguori
ONE LIGUORI DRIVE
LIGUORI MO 63057-9999

# Dedication

To my family:
my parents Jim and Peg,
my husband Bill,
our son Sam and daughter-in-law Erin,
and our precious grandchildren
Ben, Lucas, and Andrew

To all the children I have had the privilege of
teaching throughout the years.

*Imprimi Potest:*
Harry Grile, CSsR, Provincial
Denver Province, The Redemptorists

Published by Liguori Publications
Liguori, Missouri 63057

To order, call 800-325-9521
www.liguori.org

p ISBN 978-0-7648-2294-0
e ISBN 978-0-7648-6913-6

Liguori Publications, a nonprofit corporation, is an apostolate of The Redemptorists. To learn more about The Redemptorists, visit Redemptorists.com.

Printed in the United States of America
18 17 16 15 14  /  5 4 3 2 1
First Edition

# Dear Parents and Teachers:

*Saints and Me!* is a series of children's books about saints, with six books in each set. The first set, *Saints of North America,* honors holy men and women who blessed and served the land we call home. The second set, *Saints of Christmas,* includes heavenly heroes who inspire us through Advent and Christmas and teach us to love the Infant Jesus.

*Saints for Families* introduces the virtuous lives of seven saints from different times and places who modeled God's love and charity within and for families. Saint Thérèse of Lisieux felt the love of her family and carried it into her religious community (which included her sisters). Saint Anthony of Padua is the patron of infants and children. Saint John Bosco cared for young, homeless boys, raising them like sons. Saint Thomas More, a father of five, imitated Christ's sacrificial love and devotion to the truth until death. Saints Joachim and Anne became the grandparents of Jesus, raising Mary as a sinless disciple. And Saint Gerard Majella, the patron of pregnant mothers, blessed families with food, knowledge, penances, and healing miracles.

Which saint stood up against a king? Who became a tailor and priest? Which saint is "the little flower?" Who was known for his excellent preaching? Which saints lived before Jesus? Which saint climbed trees, did flips, and turned cartwheels? Find out in the *Saints for Families* set—part of the *Saints and Me!* series—and help your child connect to the lives of the saints.

Introduce your children or students to the *Saints and Me!* series as they:

—READ about the lives of the saints and are inspired by their stories.

—PRAY to the saints for their intercession.

—CELEBRATE the saints and relate to their lives.

**John Bosco**
**1815–1888**
**Born:** Becchi, Italy

**Joachim and Anne**
**First century BC**
**Born:** Nazareth (Joachim) Bethlehem (Anne)

**Anthony of Padua**
**1195–1231**
**Born:** Lisbon, Portugal

Gerard Majella
1726–1755
**Born:** Muro, Italy

Thérèse of Lisieux
1873–1897
**Born:** Alençon, France

Thomas More
1478–1535
**Born:** London, England

Thomas More was born in London, England. He liked to study and learn new things. Thomas was a good student and had many friends. Children enjoyed playing with Thomas because he was funny and kind.

For a time, he stayed at the home of the archbishop of Canterbury. It was an exciting place. He met many important people there. Thomas learned how to help people and listen to them. "You are a fine young man," the archbishop told Thomas.

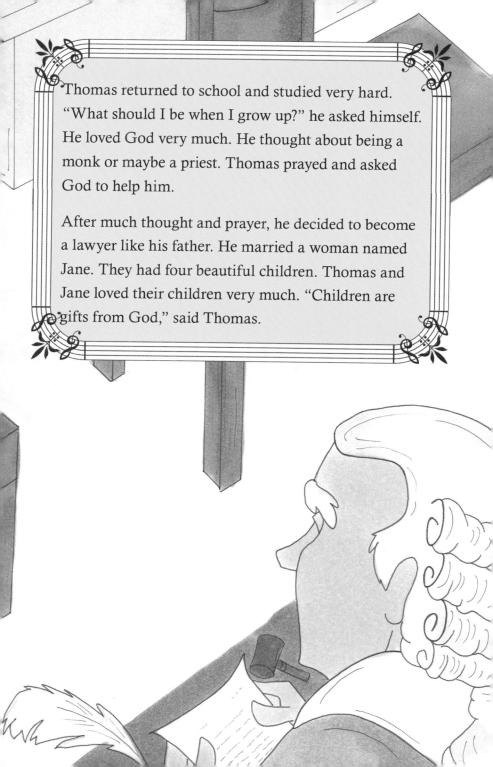

Thomas returned to school and studied very hard. "What should I be when I grow up?" he asked himself. He loved God very much. He thought about being a monk or maybe a priest. Thomas prayed and asked God to help him.

After much thought and prayer, he decided to become a lawyer like his father. He married a woman named Jane. They had four beautiful children. Thomas and Jane loved their children very much. "Children are gifts from God," said Thomas.

The More house was full of laughter and love.
Friends and neighbors were always welcome.
"Come, children; it is time to pray. Whose turn
is it to read from the Bible?" Thomas asked.
Margaret, the oldest daughter, smiled and said, "It
is my turn, Father." Thomas gave her the Bible.

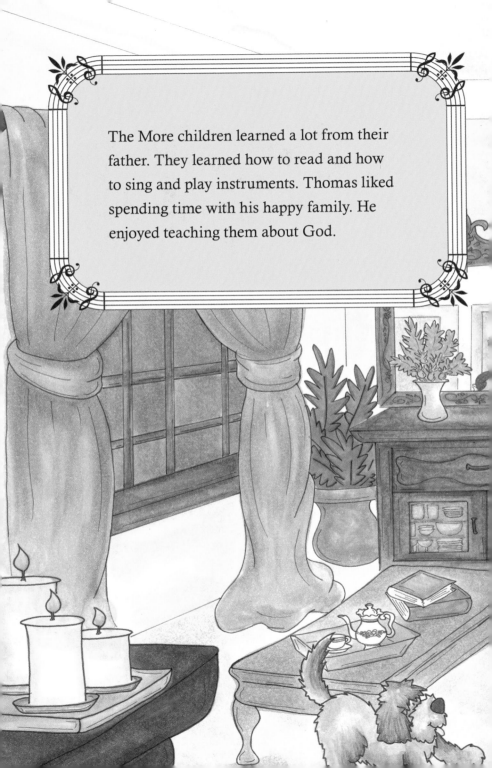

The More children learned a lot from their father. They learned how to read and how to sing and play instruments. Thomas liked spending time with his happy family. He enjoyed teaching them about God.

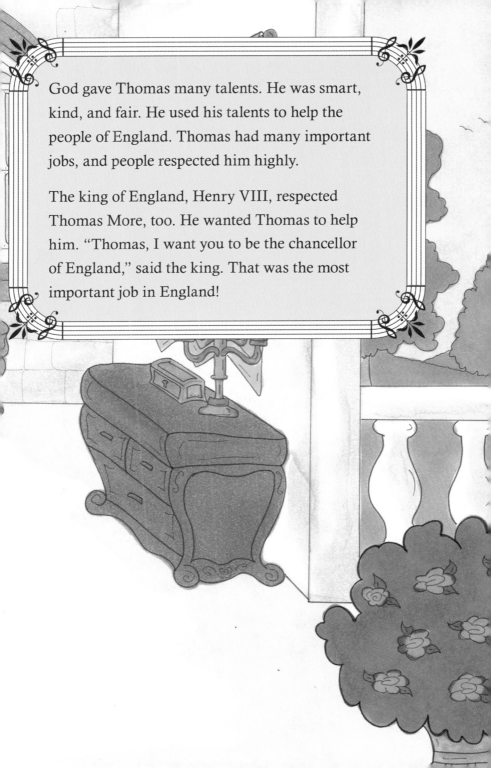

God gave Thomas many talents. He was smart, kind, and fair. He used his talents to help the people of England. Thomas had many important jobs, and people respected him highly.

The king of England, Henry VIII, respected Thomas More, too. He wanted Thomas to help him. "Thomas, I want you to be the chancellor of England," said the king. That was the most important job in England!

But soon things changed. King Henry VIII decided he wanted things for himself. He wanted power. "I want people to obey me. I want to be head of the Church," said the king. "The pope is the head of the Church," Thomas told him. King Henry was not happy.

The king made a new law. People had to take an oath, or special promise. Taking the oath meant you agreed that King Henry VIII was the head of the Church of England. If you did not take the oath, you would be put in prison. Thomas was very sad.

"Thomas, you are my friend," said King
Henry. "Yes, but I serve God and the
Church first. The pope is the head of the
Church. You are not the pope," Thomas
said softly.

Thomas left his job as the chancellor of England. He could not take the oath. It was not right. "I believe strongly in the laws of the Church," sighed Thomas. Thomas knew his decision would cause many problems.

Thomas went to live at his home in the country. It was peaceful and quiet. He could read and write there. He enjoyed spending time with his family. They lived life more simply now, but they were happy being together.

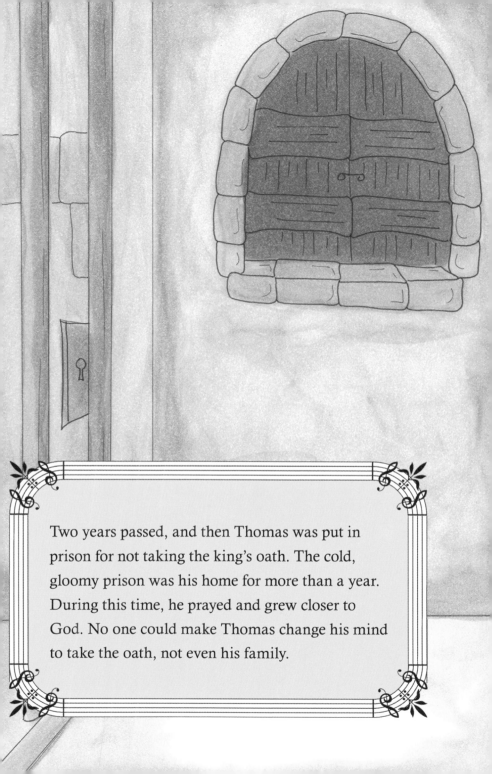

Two years passed, and then Thomas was put in prison for not taking the king's oath. The cold, gloomy prison was his home for more than a year. During this time, he prayed and grew closer to God. No one could make Thomas change his mind to take the oath, not even his family.

When it was time for his trial, he was found guilty of treason—not being loyal to his country. The punishment was death. Thomas More died on July 6, 1535—a martyr for the faith.

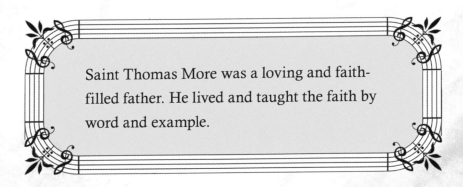

Saint Thomas More was a loving and faith-filled father. He lived and taught the faith by word and example.

*Whatever you do,*
*Be faithful and true.*

Dear god.

I love you.

saint Thomas more

loved you and

the church.

help me to put god

first in my life.

give me the courage

to stand up for

what is right.

Amen.

# NEW WORDS (Glossary)

**Archbishop:** A bishop who is the leader of many churches in a large or important area

**Chancellor of England:** A person who works with the courts and laws of England. It is an important job in England's government.

**Guilty:** Having done something that is wrong or that breaks a law

**Lawyer:** Someone who gives legal advice and sometimes stands up for someone in court

**Martyr:** A person who is put to death for the faith

**Monk:** A man who lives in a religious community in a monastery, a quiet place to pray and think

**Oath:** A serious promise or pledge

**Respect:** Honor that a person gives to another

**Treason:** The crime of not being loyal to your country

A play about Saint Thomas More called *A Man for All Seasons* has been performed around the world. The movie with the same title won many awards.

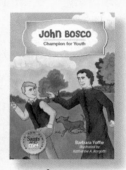